KEEP YOUR DINOSAURS HERE

Sabrina Ricci

I KNOW DINO

Keep Your Dinosaurs Here: 100 Creative Journal Prompts for Dinosaur Enthusiasts

Copyright © 2016 Sabrina Ricci

Published by I Know Dino, LLC

Notebook Cover Image © 2016 Seregam, used under license from Shutterstock.com
Guerrilla font designed by Carlos Zubia
Additional images from Shutterstock.com and publicdomainvectors.org

ISBN: 153075822X
ISBN-13: 978-1530758227

DINOSAURS BRING PEOPLE TOGETHER.

WHAT'S YOUR FAVORITE MOMENT INVOLVING A DINOSAUR? WHO ELSE WAS THERE?

....

....

....

....

....

....

....

....

....

....

....

....

....

....

....

....

WHAT WOULD YOU ASK A PALEONTOLOGIST?

PROJECT: **WRITE THEM A LETTER OR EMAIL.**

WHAT DINOSAUR MOVIES DO YOU LIKE WATCHING WITH FRIENDS?

LIST YOUR 5 FAVORITE DINOSAUR MOVIES HERE.

WHICH DINOSAUR MAKES YOU SMILE?

SKETCH DRAW YOUR FAVORITE DINOSAUR HERE. (DOES IT HAVE FEATHERS?)

IF YOU HAD 2 WEEKS TO GO ON A ROAD TRIP, WHERE WOULD YOU GO? WHAT DINOSAURS WOULD YOU VISIT? BRAINSTORM YOUR ITINERARY HERE.

IF YOU COULD BE ANY KIND OF DINOSAUR, WHAT WOULD YOU BE? WOULD YOU LIVE ON LAND OR WOULD YOU BE ABLE TO FLY?

....

....

....

....

....

....

....

....

....

....

....

....

....

....

....

....

DESIGN A DINOSAUR COSTUME.

PROJECT: MAKE IT AND WEAR IT
THIS HALLOWEEN.

NOW DESIGN A COSTUME FOR YOU AND A FRIEND. MAKE A THEME OUT OF IT.

CHALLENGE: THROW A DINOSAUR THEMED PARTY.

WHAT'S THE CRAZIEST FACT YOU KNOW ABOUT DINOSAURS?

....

....

....

....

....

....

....

....

....

....

....

....

....

BONUS: SHARE YOUR FACT WITH A FRIEND.

STEGOSAURUS MAY HAVE BEEN ABLE TO SWIM. SKETCH WHAT THAT WOULD'VE LOOKED LIKE.

MAKE A LIST OF YOUR 5 FAVORITE DINOSAUR BOOKS.

....

....

....

....

....

IF YOU COULD NAME A DINOSAUR, WHAT WOULD YOU NAME IT? HOW DID YOU COME UP WITH THAT NAME?

....

....

....

....

....

....

....

....

....

....

....

....

....

....

IF YOU COULD ASK A CARNIVOROUS DINOSAUR ANY QUESTION, WHAT WOULD IT BE?

How much do you know?

List the top 10 biggest dinosaurs discovered so far.

....

....

....

....

....

....

....

....

....

....

....

....

....

....

....

....

....

....

....

....

....

....

PRETEND YOU WORK AT A MUSEUM, AND YOU HAVE THE OPPORTUNITY TO PLAN A MUSEUM EXHIBIT. WHICH DINOSAURS ARE IN IT? (SKETCH HERE.)

SKETCH

THE WATER IN YOUR BODY WAS ONCE PART OF A DINOSAUR. WRITE A SHORT STORY ABOUT HOW THAT WATER GOT THERE.

IF YOU COULD OWN 3 LIFE-SIZED DINOSAUR STATUES, WHAT WOULD THEY BE? WHAT WOULD YOU DO WITH THEM? (PLAY A PRANK? SET UP A MINI-MUSEUM? THE POSSIBILITIES ARE ENDLESS!)

....

....

....

....

....

....

....

....

....

....

....

WRITE A LETTER TO AN AUTHOR WHO WROTE A DINOSAUR BOOK. WHAT DID YOU LEARN FROM THE BOOK THAT YOU WOULDN'T HAVE KNOWN OTHERWISE?

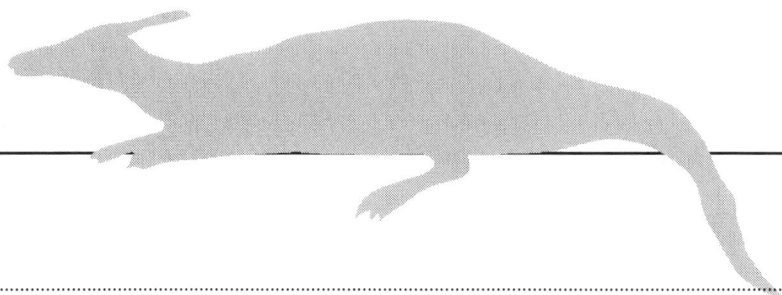

YOU CAN HAVE A DINOSAUR AS A PET. WHICH DO YOU CHOOSE AND WHY?

WHICH DINOSAUR WOULD MAKE THE WORST PET?

WOULD YOU RATHER BE A CARNIVOROUS DINOSAUR OR AN HERBIVOROUS DINOSAUR?

LIST 5 REASONS WHY.

SPINOSAURUS HAD A SAIL. WHAT DO YOU THINK IT USED ITS SAIL FOR?

SKETCH A *SPINOSAURUS* USING ITS SAIL.

Do you prefer realistic dinosaur drawings or cartoon-ish dinosaur drawings? Why?

TECHNOLOGY KEEPS IMPROVING, AND EACH YEAR WE LEARN MORE AND MORE ABOUT DINOSAURS. WHAT DO YOU THINK WE'LL KNOW ABOUT DINOSAURS 50 YEARS FROM NOW THAT WE DON'T KNOW ALREADY?

WHAT DO YOU THINK WE'LL KNOW ABOUT DINOSAURS 100 YEARS FROM NOW?

CAMPTOSAURUS WAS A PLANT EATING ORNITHISCHIAN THAT HAD A THUMB SPIKE, BUT IT WAS TOO SMALL TO USE FOR DEFENSE. WHAT DO YOU THINK *CAMPTOSAURUS* USED THE THUMB SPIKE FOR?

WHICH DINOSAUR MOVIE INSPIRES YOU? WRITE DOWN WHY HERE.

....

....

....

....

....

....

....

....

....

....

....

....

....

....

....

IF YOU COULD MAKE A DINOSAUR MOVIE, WHAT WOULD IT BE ABOUT?

DRAW A POSTER FOR THE MOVIE.

WRITE DOWN YOUR WISH LIST OF DINOSAUR SITES TO SEE.

☐ ....

☐ ....

☐ ....

☐ ....

☐ ....

☐ ....

☐ ....

☐ ....

☐ ....

☐ ....

☐ ....

☐ ....

☐ ....

☐ ....

☐ ....

PROJECT: START VISITING THOSE SITES AND CHECK THEM OFF, ONE BY ONE!

WOULD YOU RATHER BE A BIG DINOSAUR OR A SMALL DINOSAUR? (FOR EXAMPLE, AN *ALLOSAURUS* OR A *COMPSOGNATHUS*?)

....

....

....

....

....

....

....

....

....

....

....

....

....

....

....

....

....

IF YOU COULD ASK AN HERBIVOROUS DINOSAUR ANY QUESTION, WHAT WOULD IT BE?

YOU'VE BEEN TRANSPORTED TO THE
CRETACEOUS. A *T. REX* IS CHASING
YOU. WHAT KIND OF GETAWAY VEHICLE
WOULD YOU NEED OR WANT?

SKETCH DRAW THE SCENE HERE.

IF A DINOSAUR WAS CHASING YOU,
WOULD IT BE BETTER TO ESCAPE ON
A BOAT, PLANE, OR CAR?
REMEMBER, IN THE MESOZOIC ERA
PLESIOSAURS LIVED IN WATER AND
PTEROSAURS COULD FLY.

IF *TRICERATOPS* DIDN'T GO EXTINCT AND CONTINUED TO EVOLVE, HOW DO YOU THINK IT WOULD HAVE LOOKED?

LIST **SKETCH** LIST 5 FEATURES AND THEN SKETCH HERE.

THE SOUNDS OF *T. REX* IN THE MOVIE *JURASSIC PARK* WERE A MIX OF WHALE, ELEPHANT, TIGER, AND ALLIGATOR NOISES. HOW DO YOU THINK *T. REX* ACTUALLY SOUNDED?

....

....

....

....

....

....

....

....

....

....

....

....

....

WHAT WOULD YOU DO IF YOU CAME FACE-TO-FACE WITH A DINOSAUR?

....

....

....

....

....

....

....

....

....

....

IF YOU HAD TO HUNT AND EAT A DINOSAUR, WHICH ONE WOULD YOU GO AFTER?

WHICH DINOSAUR DO YOU THINK TASTED THE BEST?

....

....

....

....

....

....

....

....

....

....

....

....

....

....

"FOSSILS HAVE RICHER STORIES TO TELL – ABOUT THE LUB-DUB OF DINOSAUR LIFE – THAN WE HAVE BEEN WILLING TO LISTEN TO."

-ROBERT T. BAKKER

WHAT DO YOU THINK WE'VE MISSED FROM FOSSILS SO FAR?

....

....

....

....

....

....

....

....

....

....

....

....

....

....

....

....

....

IF *ANKYLOSAURUS* DIDN'T GO EXTINCT AND CONTINUED TO EVOLVE, HOW DO YOU THINK IT WOULD HAVE LOOKED?

LIST 5 FEATURES AND THEN SKETCH HERE.

LIST

SKETCH

LIST YOUR TOP 10 DINOSAUR MUSEUMS.

....

....

....

....

....

....

....

....

....

....

IF YOU WERE GOING TO CREATE A NEW DINOSAUR, WHAT KIND OF DINOSAUR WOULD IT BE?

 **DESCRIBE ITS FEATURES AND SKETCH YOUR DINOSAUR HERE.**

How do you think dinosaurs communicated?

....

....

....

....

....

....

....

....

....

....

....

SCIENTISTS HAVE RECREATED HOW *PARASAUROLOPHUS* MAY HAVE SOUNDED, USING CT SCANS. THEY FOUND THAT *PARASAUROLOPHUS* MADE LOW FREQUENCY HONKING NOISES.

SKETCH A *PARASAUROLOPHUS* CALLING TO ITS MATE.

WOULD YOU RATHER BE A DINOSAUR, PTEROSAUR, OR AN ANCIENT MARINE REPTILE?

GIVE 3 REASONS WHY.

_____

_____

_____

_____

_____

_____

_____

_____

_____

_____

_____

_____

_____

_____

VERSUS

WHO DO YOU THINK WOULD WIN IN A FIGHT BETWEEN *T. REX* AND *TRICERATOPS?*

SKETCH **DRAW THE BATTLE HERE.**

WE DON'T KNOW WHAT COLORS
DINOSAURS WERE BECAUSE MOST
COLORS DON'T FOSSILIZE.

 SKETCH A DINOSAUR HERE AND
COLOR IN HOW YOU THINK IT
LOOKED.

IF YOU COULD VISIT ANY DINOSAUR QUARRY OR DIG SITE, WHICH ONE WOULD IT BE? WHAT WOULD YOU HOPE TO FIND?

BASED ON DINOSAUR BONE STRUCTURE, SCIENTISTS BELIEVE DINOSAURS LIVED TO BE BETWEEN 75 AND 300 YEARS OLD.

WRITE A BUCKET LIST FOR A 300-YEAR-OLD DINOSAUR.

LIST

YOU'RE LOCKED IN A NATURAL HISTORY MUSEUM FOR THE NIGHT. YOU HAVE THE ENTIRE NIGHT TO DO WHATEVER YOU WANT IN THE MUSEUM. HOW DO YOU SPEND IT?

ANKYLOSAURUS MAY HAVE BEEN ABLE TO BLUSH. WHAT MIGHT CAUSE IT TO BLUSH?

WRITE A SHORT STORY HERE.

SKETCH SOME SCIENTISTS ARE FIGURING OUT HOW TO TURN A CHICKEN INTO A DINOSAUR. WHAT DO YOU THINK A CHICKENOSAURUS WOULD LOOK LIKE? SKETCH IT HERE.

WHICH PALEONTOLOGISTS DO YOU MOST ADMIRE? WHY?

IF YOU COULD BE ANY DINOSAUR, WHICH DINOSAUR WOULD YOU BE? DESCRIBE A TYPICAL DAY AS THAT DINOSAUR HERE.

WHAT'S THE BEST DINOSAUR JOKE YOU'VE HEARD? SHARE IT HERE. OR MAKE ONE UP.

CHALLENGE: TELL YOUR JOKE TO A FRIEND!

TO DO

You visit a natural history museum and have the chance to meet the museum curator. You are allowed to ask 1 question. What would you most like to know about dinosaurs?

CHALLENGE: REACH OUT TO A PALEONTOLOGIST OR MUSEUM CURATOR AND ASK YOUR QUESTION.

TO DO

IF YOU COULD MAKE ANY LIFE-SIZED ANIMATRONIC DINOSAUR, WHICH ONE WOULD IT BE? WHY?

IF *T. REX* DIDN'T GO EXTINCT AND CONTINUED TO EVOLVE, HOW DO YOU THINK IT WOULD HAVE LOOKED?

LIST

SKETCH

LIST 5 FEATURES AND THEN SKETCH HERE.

VERSUS

WHO DO YOU THINK WOULD WIN IN A FIGHT BETWEEN *SPINOSAURUS* AND *T. REX*?

SKETCH **DRAW THE BATTLE HERE.**

"I THINK MOST OF THE DINOSAUR SPECIMENS WE FIND REPRESENT SUBADULT SIZES."

-JACK HORNER

WHAT DO YOU THINK? IF MOST DINOSAURS WE'VE FOUND WERE NOT FULLY GROWN, HOW BIG DO YOU THINK THEY COULD BECOME?

....

....

....

....

....

....

....

....

....

....

....

....

....

HOW MUCH DO YOU KNOW?

LIST THE TOP 10 SMALLEST DINOSAURS DISCOVERED SO FAR.

....

....

....

....

....

....

....

....

....

....

....

....

....

....

WRITE A LETTER TO A DIRECTOR WHO MADE A DINOSAUR MOVIE. WHAT ABOUT THAT MOVIE INSPIRED YOU?

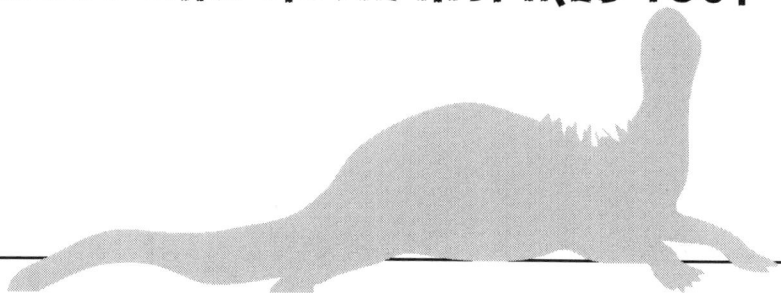

Fun Facts

The Cleveland-Lloyd Dinosaur Quarry has over 12,000 dinosaur bones from the Jurassic period.

About 75% of them are carnivore bones, mostly *Allosaurus*.

Scientists have yet to solve the mystery of how so many dinosaurs, especially predators, ended up at that quarry.

Some hypotheses include:
- a death trap,
- drought,
- poisoning,
- and "bloat and float"—where a dinosaur died somewhere else and its body was carried downstream to the quarry.

What do you think happened at the Cleveland-Lloyd Dinosaur Quarry?

....

....

....

....

....

....

....

....

....

....

....

....

....

....

....

....

....

....

....

....

....

....

....

STEGOSAURUS HAD GIANT PLATES
ON ITS BACK. WHAT DO YOU THINK
WAS THE PURPOSE OF THOSE
PLATES?

SKETCH A STEGOSAURUS HERE
USING ITS PLATES.

THE FASTEST DINOSAURS WERE THE BIRD-LIKE ORNITHOMIMIDS, AND SOME COULD RUN UP TO 37 MPH (~60 KPH).

SKETCH A RUNNING ORNITHOMIMID HERE.

If you could travel back in time to the Mesozoic era, which period would you choose? Triassic? Jurassic? Cretaceous?

....

....

....

....

....

....

....

....

....

....

....

....

....

....

....

....

....

....

....

....

....

....

....

IMAGINE EARLY HUMANS WERE AROUND WHEN NON-AVIAN DINOSAURS STILL EXISTED. HOW WOULD HUMANS HAVE TREATED DINOSAURS? WOULD THEY HAVE TRIED TO DOMESTICATE THEM? HUNT THEM? BOTH? WHAT WOULD LIFE HAVE BEEN LIKE?

VERSUS

WHO DO YOU THINK WOULD WIN IN A FIGHT BETWEEN *T. REX* AND *VELOCIRAPTOR*?

SKETCH **DRAW THE BATTLE HERE.**

NOT MUCH IS KNOWN ABOUT DINOSAURS THAT LIVED IN MOUNTAINS.

SKETCH WHAT YOU THINK THEY MAY HAVE LOOKED LIKE.

IF DINOSAURS WERE AROUND, WHICH ONES WOULD YOU LIKE TO MEET? (WOULD YOU MEET A FAMILY OF DINOSAURS OR WOULD YOU PREFER TO MEET A SINGLE DINOSAUR?)

....

....

....

....

....

....

....

....

....

....

....

....

WRITE A SHORT STORY ABOUT DINOSAURS. NO LIMITS!

WHAT WOULD YOU MOST LIKE TO LEARN OR HOPE SCIENTISTS LEARN ABOUT DINOSAURS IN THE FUTURE?

....

....

....

....

....

....

....

....

....

....

....

....

....

....

....

....

....

....

YOU HAVE THE OPPORTUNITY TO BRING A DINOSAUR BACK FROM EXTINCTION. WHICH DINOSAUR DO YOU PICK? WHY?

YOU GET TO GO ON A DIG WITH A PALEONTOLOGIST. WHERE DO YOU GO? WHAT DO YOU HOPE TO FIND?

WRITE YOUR DAY 1 JOURNAL ENTRY HERE.

JURASSIC PARK HAS INSPIRED A WHOLE GENERATION OF PALEONTOLOGISTS. WHAT HAS INSPIRED YOU AS A DINOSAUR ENTHUSIAST?

....

....

....

....

....

....

....

....

....

....

....

....

....

....

....

VERSUS

WHO DO YOU THINK WOULD WIN IN A FIGHT BETWEEN *ALLOSAURUS* AND *APATOSAURUS?*

DRAW THE BATTLE HERE.

HOW BIG WAS A SAUROPOD HERD?

 SKETCH A HERD HERE.

FUN FACT

DIPLODOCUS WAS CATHEMERAL, WHICH MEANS IT WOKE UP AND SLEPT WHENEVER IT WANTED, NO MATTER WHAT TIME OF DAY.

WRITE A STORY ABOUT A TYPICAL DAY FOR *DIPLODOCUS.*

WHAT'S ONE OF THE BIGGEST MYSTERIES ABOUT DINOSAURS?

....

....

....

....

....

....

....

....

....

....

....

....

....

....

....

MAKE A LIST OF YOUR FAVORITE DINOSAUR TRAITS.

IF *PACHYCEPHALOSAURUS* DIDN'T GO EXTINCT AND CONTINUED TO EVOLVE, HOW DO YOU THINK IT WOULD HAVE LOOKED?

LIST 5 FEATURES AND THEN SKETCH HERE.

TRIASSIC DINOSAURS WERE SMALL. WRITE A STORY OF WHAT IT WOULD BE LIKE TO BE A SMALL DINOSAUR IN THE TRIASSIC, BEFORE DINOSAURS RULED THE WORLD.

NOW WRITE A STORY OF WHAT IT WAS LIKE WHEN DINOSAURS WERE BIGGER AND AT THE TOP OF THE FOOD CHAIN.

ARE YOU THINKING OF GOING INTO A CAREER THAT INVOLVES DINOSAURS? WHO WOULD YOU ASK FOR ADVICE?

....

....

....

....

....

....

....

....

....

....

....

....

....

WRITE A LIST OF ALL THE PEOPLE WHO HAVE SUPPORTED YOUR DINOSAUR OBSESSION.

VERSUS

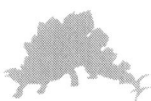

WHO DO YOU THINK WOULD WIN IN A FIGHT BETWEEN *CERATOSAURUS* AND *STEGOSAURUS*?

SKETCH **DRAW THE BATTLE HERE.**

IF *DAKOTARAPTOR* DIDN'T GO EXTINCT AND CONTINUED TO EVOLVE, HOW DO YOU THINK IT WOULD HAVE LOOKED?

LIST 5 FEATURES AND THEN SKETCH HERE.

SCIENTISTS HAVE FOUND SOME EVIDENCE THAT DINOSAURS ATE PLANTS THAT WOULD HAVE MADE THEM HALLUCINATE. WHAT HIJINKS WOULD ENSUE? HOW WOULD A HACCULINATING DINOSAUR ACT? WRITE A SHORT STORY HERE.

....

....

....

....

....

....

....

....

....

....

....

....

....

....

....

....

....

MOST BABY DINOSAURS HAD
PROPORTIONALLY LARGER EYES
AND SMALLER FACES THAN
ADULTS, WHICH MADE THEM JUST
AS CUTE AS OTHER BABY ANIMALS.

 SKETCH A CUTE BABY DINOSAUR.

If you could go anywhere on a dinosaur dig, where would you go?

....

....

....

....

....

....

....

....

....

....

....

....

....

....

....

....

....

....

....

....

....

....

WHAT DO YOU THINK THE WORLD WOULD BE LIKE IF NON-AVIAN DINOSAURS LIVED TODAY?

MAIASAURA IS A DUCK-BILLED DINOSAUR KNOWN AS THE "GOOD MOTHER."

 SKETCH *MAIASAURA* TENDING TO HER YOUNG.

WHAT'S THE HARDEST DINOSAUR NAME TO PRONOUNCE? MAKE A TONGUE TWISTER OUT OF IT.

YOU HAVE THE CHANCE TO DIRECT A DINOSAUR MOVIE. WHAT KIND OF DINOSAURS DO YOU INCLUDE? WHAT HAPPENS IN YOUR MOVIE? WHERE DOES IT TAKE PLACE? WRITE YOUR STORY IDEA HERE.

....

....

....

....

....

....

....

....

....

....

....

....

....

Fun Facts

Deinocheirus mirificus is a dinosaur that mystified paleontologists for 50 years, when they only knew about its giant arms.

Then in 2014 the rest of its body was found, and it turned out to be a bizarre dinosaur, with
A DUCK-LIKE BEAK,
A BIG HUMPED SAIL ON ITS BACK,
HOOVES ON ITS FEET,
AND A BIG GUT.

Some have likened it to Jar Jar Binks from *Star Wars*.

SKETCH *DEINOCHEIRUS* HERE.

WHAT IS IT ABOUT DINOSAURS THAT MAKE THEM SO FASCINATING TO YOU?

....

....

....

....

....

....

....

....

....

....

....

....

....

CHALLENGE: POST YOUR STORY TO I KNOW DINO ON FACEBOOK.

DINOSAURS EVOLVED INTO BIRDS. SKETCH THE PROCESS.

SKETCH

WRITE A DINOSAUR HAIKU.
HAIKUS ARE COMPOSED OF 3
LINES.
THE FIRST LINE HAS 5 SYLLABLES,
THE SECOND LINE HAS 7 SYLLABLES,
AND THE THIRD LINE HAS 5 SYLLABLES.

MAKE A LIST OF DINOSAUR FACTS OR QUOTES YOU HEARD THIS WEEK THAT MADE YOU SMILE.

DESCRIBE A SPECIAL MEMORY YOU HAVE WITH A FRIEND OR FAMILY MEMBER AT A NATURAL HISTORY MUSEUM, OR ANOTHER EXPERIENCE INVOLVING DINOSAURS. WHAT MADE THAT DAY SO MEMORABLE FOR YOU?

....

....

....

....

....

....

....

....

....

....

....

....

....

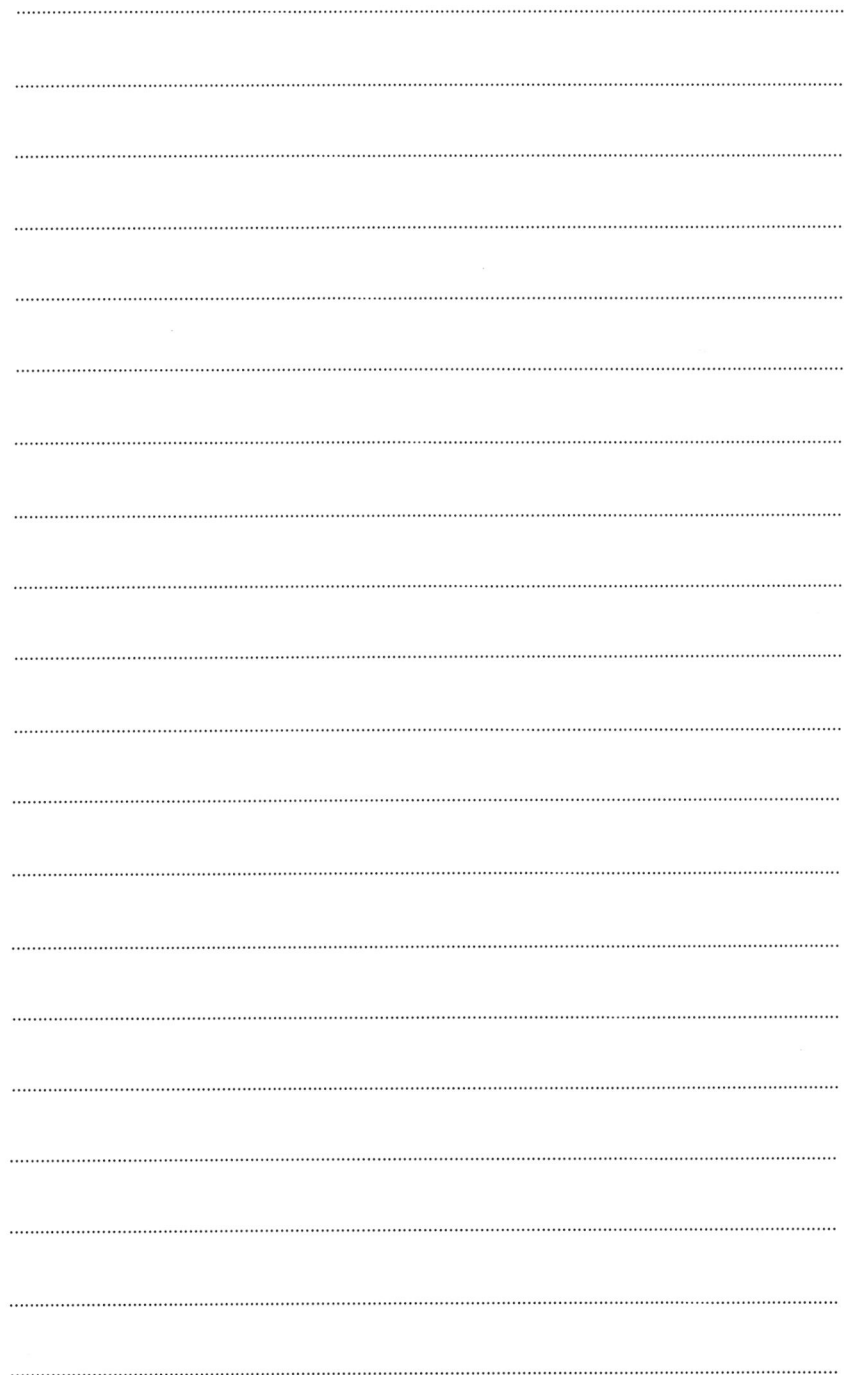

THANK YOU!

My deepest thanks to all the dinosaur enthusiasts out there. I hope you get a lot out of this journal.

Sabrina is a writer and podcaster. She loves nerdy things, like technical specs and dinosaurs, especially sauropods. When she's not writing, she's podcasting with her husband at *I Know Dino* (iknowdino.com), a weekly show about dinosaurs.

FOR DINOSAUR ENTHUSIASTS

Are you really into dinosaurs? Sign up to the I Know Dino mailing list at iknowdino.com for news, updates, and special offers on all upcoming dinosaur books.

CONNECT WITH SABRINA VIA I KNOW DINO

Website: https://iknowdino.com
iTunes: https://itunes.apple.com/us/podcast/i-know-dino-big-dinosaur-podcast/id960976813
Instagram: https://www.instagram.com/iknowdino
YouTube: https://www.youtube.com/c/iknowdino
Tumblr: http://iknowdino.tumblr.com
Facebook: https://www.facebook.com/iknowdino
Twitter: https://twitter.com/IKnowDino
TikTok: https://www.tiktok.com/@iknowdino
Pinterest: https://www.pinterest.com/iknowdino
LinkedIn: https://www.linkedin.com/company/i-know-dino
Patreon: https://www.patreon.com/iknowdino

WANT MORE DINOSAURS?

CHECK OUT THESE OTHER BOOKS BY I KNOW DINO:

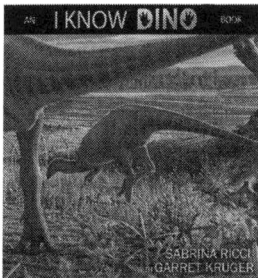

AN I KNOW **DINO** BOOK
50 DINOSAUR TALES
SABRINA RICCI GARRET KRUGER
AND 108 MORE DISCOVERIES FROM THE GOLDEN AGE OF DINOS

AN I KNOW **DINO** BOOK
TOP 10 DINOSAURS OF 2017
BY SABRINA RICCI
THE 10 BIGGEST DINOSAUR DISCOVERIES OF 2017

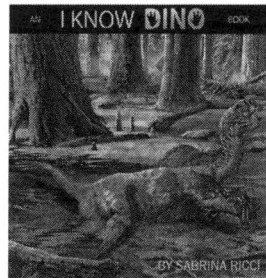

AN I KNOW **DINO** BOOK
TOP 10 DINOSAURS OF 2016
BY SABRINA RICCI
THE 10 BIGGEST DINOSAUR DISCOVERIES OF 2016

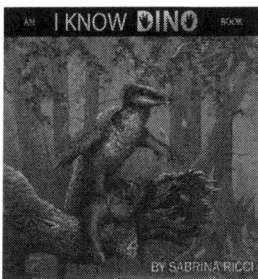

AN I KNOW **DINO** BOOK
TOP 10 DINOSAURS OF 2015
BY SABRINA RICCI
THE 10 BIGGEST DINOSAUR DISCOVERIES OF 2015

What Happened to *Brontosaurus*?
written by Sabrina Ricci illustrated by Gagyi Pelffy Andrea

AN I KNOW **DINO** BOOK
TOP 10 DINOSAURS OF 2014
BY SABRINA RICCI
THE 10 BIGGEST DINOSAUR DISCOVERIES OF 2014

Made in United States
Orlando, FL
14 January 2023